Grief Slut

Sundress Publications • Knoxville, TN

Copyright © 2024 by Evelyn Berry
ISBN: 978-1-951979-54-6
Library of Congress: 2023945634
Published by Sundress Publications
www.sundresspublications.com

Book Editor: Erin Elizabeth Smith
Managing Editor: Tennison S. Black
Editorial Assistant: Kanika Lawton
Editorial Interns: Izzy Astuto, Heather Domenicis, Jen Gayda Gupta

Colophon: This book is set in Bembo Std.

Cover Image: "Wounded + Hopeful" by Silas Bird

Cover Design: Kristen Ton

Author Photo: Jared Johnson

Book Design: Erin Elizabeth Smith

Grief Slut

Evelyn Berry

Table of Contents

Part 3

Part 4

"There is no / somewhere over a rainbow, somewhere / a place for us. This is the place." –Ed Madden

praise song
in lieu of obituary

bless the tenor in my chest cajoling song
from cement mixer. bless the sprigs of
coarse hair sprouting from my nipples.
bless the burlap skin, bless the razor
scraped across my chin, bruised stubble.
this body that has carried me, bless it all,
even what i'd rather abandon.

bless this sugar-wrecked relic, rust-
feathered myth in my blood. bless this
bouquet of bruise & belly fat!

bless my body, prelude to a corpse,
prologue to whatever comes next. bless
the boy born here. bless my body for
holding my body long enough to
imagine a future. derek, silly, sweet
derek. bless this body not because it is
beautiful but because it is mine.

Part 1

queer the smear

behind
the school,
we scrum.
we bum rush.
we hum
the slur,
sing
for brief
carnage.
we drum
skin red,
become
bruisenumb.
we limpwrist
launch
the football
above us,
spread arms
to catch
its descent.
we thrum
with violence.
we come
undone.

no rules
except blood
glitzing grass,
parking lot
gravel sparkling
in sunlight
like glitter.

there is no other way
boys may touch,
may hold each other
against the dirt.

the third day

we cheese with missing teeth,
brothers in matching buzzcuts
& easter suits like miniature
pastors. in the churchyard,
we scour the grass for eggs
peeking vibrant from hiding spots.
in the pews, we gorge silent
on chocolate squares & stare,
reverent, at the suffering christ
wire-hoisted above the pulpit.
he keeps dying & coming back
each year, like a goldfish
your parents have secretly flushed
& replaced with a brother
who shares the same name.

we've got wilderness
stuck in our teeth

maws crammed
with dead leaves,
frog limbs, secret
treasure maps
scrawled on the undersides
of our tongues.

we are brothers.
we are feral
scab eaters,
sugar-buzzed
& drunk
on each other's
violent spit.
we crash our bikes
on purpose.
my brothers,
my brothers,
we swallow grease
abundant, heir
to everything
that bleeds easy,
all that when pinned
beneath a magnifying lens
will burn.

once, bats
flooded the attic,
erratic colony
of night's music.
at dusk, we hung
a bucket of honey

outside the window.
they evacuated
the house & rose
into the sky,
then the bucket filled
with their screaming.
the still living wheeled
above the roof,
silent gliders.
we raised guns.
we took aim.

summer of the push mower

& the mediocre slash-job
i perform for house owners

on the lower portions of their backyards,
where they cannot spy how i've shorn the grass

like a child's head who forgets to speak back properly
to his father after opening his eyes during prayer.

wreathed in sweat, i march and schlep
the mower, its motor sputtering like skillet grease.

i beseech neighbors for ten dollars
to defile their lawns with rust-baptized blades.

all that's left behind are dandelions
growing too close to stumps and shallow ditches.

i mourn to raze anything that grows so wild.

i'm seven when i dredge a cold body
from the creek

below graniteville mill,
i dislodge a small hook
from a gasping mouth.

we keep the papermouths
in a foam bucket
beside the ice chest.

i wipe fish guts
on my jeans
& collapse

against the dead-grass
shore, wait to wrestle
the plastic rod again.

a school of dazzled,
dull captives dance
in the water dyed brown

with blood & squirm
to gulp bright rubber worms
waltzing below the surface.

years later, a train crashes & leaks chlorine gas.
a woman suffocates alone.
they carry her cold body
from the house below the mill.

home is what we swallow,
what soon will kill.

still

as boys, we played ball
with ruined fruit.
late spring, fallen
from the frost-brittle branches,
peaches, once crisp as parchment,
shrivel into dark orbs,
and, slammed sudden against
the errant slugger's swing,
they explode & coat our grins
sticky with regret & glee.

i've seen too many peaches rot
in the orchard to call them luxury.

in still life paintings, they glow
pink & plump, evidence of pleasure
not yet taken in the mouth.
i want to be as perfect as that:
oil-smudged fruit
framing the crab's bent claw
behind a dead pheasant
heaped on silver,
so much here alive
& not quite yet spoiled.

baptist camp for boys

entire afternoons i spent studying sweat
beading on the back of a boy's neck
at church camp, entire days praying
for light to abandon the sky.

in woodworking class, i cut my thumb.
he swallowed the fresh gash
until i stopped bleeding.

it is difficult to think summer beautiful
without imaging what happens to a peppermint
inside of a locked car, what happens to a child.

southern ecology

moss swallows
the cypress grove
easy as i devour oxy,
bone-white like frost
gone soft in the swamp heat.
to discover home, first,
one must study
the contours of loss.
nothing's left in the bog
except miller lite cans,
a crushed camel pack,
grocery bags suspended
like jellyfish glossy
with muck. once, catfish
disturbed the reed until
they plucked plastic
from the surface,
choked, then disappeared.
water now murky as memory.

the chemicals in our blood
are no invasive species.
we can be baptized & drown in the same creek.

ritual superstition

i tried to memorize prayers in other languages.
i mispronounced the name of god
until even my throat no longer belonged to me.
i launched missives at heaven, my tongue a useless catapult.
entire eras listened hard to the same silence,
their pleas, their questions, their protests
answered only by echo.

did the first prayer possess words at all?
with no written language, did we flail
in attempt to make meaning out of what a finger
might carve into dirt or how the tongue claps
against the roof of the mouth?

the first prayer must have been a blessing:
two hands pressed against the face of the dying
or cupping a dust-coated foot
or a boy still without words waking again
one summer morning to a baptism of light.

iva!

patron saint of the soft punch!
salvage yard for lost gumption!
twin roman candle, lit-wicked!

we ke$ha karaoke
until the bars close down,
thirsting like desert fruits.
we wear desire in our hair,
crowns of lavender & scavenge-bone.
we hold sparklers in our teeth.
we show each other magic tricks
we learned from the internet.
we swipe the apps, hypnotized pixeldumb,
& argue about *who's that actor in that one movie?*
           no, i mean the other one!

we wear matching
pink lipstick
to waffle house.
we sugar our coffee until lushsweet
& slurp vodka from under the table.
we devour hash browns
until our chins shine
grease-slobbed. we get sick,
& clog the drains with glitter.

we trade every story
of growing up again.
we gossipswallow & guttersnark.
we nostalgia our friends back to life.
we rumor the past into myth,
mark each memory as golden
even if we barely survived.

we survived!
remember when, do you remember, but do you—yes, yes!
friend, we have made it here together, yes!

house show

we find sanctuary in dangerous places.
when the summer becomes a sea of slurs
lashing serpent tongues against forgotten names,
we gather in a cheap apartment or crumbling house.
the music inside is louder.

we push everyone against graffiti-acned walls,
triple-sit the secondhand sofa, stack the crack-spidered
stairs with bodies. we collapse onto beds, spill cigarette
ash on the floor, kindling ready to spark.
our revelry is fleeting.
we build arks from detritus & stay afloat
just long enough to create something beautiful.

we dance with new bodies, gender-clumsy,
break them in. we break down.
we learn vocabulary
to language ourselves back to life.
we celebrate small survivals.
here, we exist.

we come to taste sweat,
to feel our feet compose
some rhythm other than running.
we come to sing poorly.
we come to feel close to something
still intact, unburned,
something bound close as blood.
we come to hear one another
breathe just a little while longer.

genderfluent

every day
shakes me loose,
doritos bag dangling
from the vending machine's
last empty coil.
every day,
i am dissolved
like a wad of gum
carried across the city
on the bottom of a boot.

every day i am tenor
singing the vehicle
of my silly little metaphors.
no, let me tell you about desire.

ha ha, just kidding.
i know nothing about desire

you cannot learn from bridging language
to the body. i know nothing of languor
i cannot learn trying, & failing,
to make sense of gender.

no, i won't explain. i'm too exhausted.

boyhood: revisions

for Derek

up, up, down, down, left, right, left right, b, a, start.[1]

he's in second grade & learns to cartwheel. he walks on his hands. he never learns to tie his shoes. he never learns to bleed without crying.[2]

at boy scout camp, he learns flint, steel wool, nest of straw & twig. he learns to build a fire. he learns a campfire song coughed through smoke. he learns to knot his brainstem. he learns to take a punch.[3]

he scrapes & scraps & scales trees. he knuckles his brother's face until his mouth bruises vermillion.[4]

he must wear the costume: cargo shorts held up by a braided belt, graphic t-shirt, dirty socks[5]

i do not want to mourn him, but i cannot let him keep living in my body.[6]

---

[1] there exists no cheat code to reverse this, to revert, to remember him as anything other than a gender-muddled boy. professor oak asks, *are you a boy or a girl?* no, i cannot remember which he picked. if anything, i've scraped memory until it is a scrapbook of convenient snapshots.

[2] he asks to sign up for gymnastics but gets placed on the football team instead, only turned upside down when colliding with the ground.

[3] to become a man, he must first arson whatever vestiges of femme he has left.

[4] no, don't say *vermillion*. primary his color palette. say, *red*. studies show women experience colors differently than men, & suddenly the hues of sunset seem too dysphoric to witness. the pills i swallow are not *blue*, but instead *periwinkle*.

[5] go ahead, tell them, i don't care: he once slipped into his friend's sister's room. he tried on her clothes. he stood in the mirror & imagined himself femme as a keychain switchblade. goddam, what a cliché! this memory is the one i point back to & say, *see, i knew then. if i can make sense of my body, it begins here.*

[6] sometimes, he feels like i'm disfiguring the family photos when i distort my voice. i retcon boyhood into illegible elegy.

i am trying to find something worth saving, something of him worth time-capsuling in the dirt of me. i swear, i do not want to forget.[7]

---

[7] here's a version of this story: once, i was a boy, then became a bird. no, once he was a mischief maker, then became a magpie. no, once he was a body until i thieved the right words for *home*. once, my mother named me for what she believed to be the last time.

Part 2

queer ecology

don't be surprised: i'm a redneck wussy
        moonshinesloppy with a limp wrist
town crier sobbing on the street corner
they'll get used to the lipstick
same like the scupadine's fleshsweet pulp
i'm here
sure as roadkill   sure as O
        possum nightslick slurping bloodticks

i'm everywhere   like a dandelion falling apart
in the wind's embrace   i'm haunting the family tree
        born to this ecology   this bloodied
patch of dirt   go ahead spit me roadside
like a boiled peanut shell sucked of salt

crown me queen of the chitlin strut

don't be surprised the ground's so fertile
young queers been fucking in the fields
since the first sin   first garden delight

first adam's apple taken in the mouth   first seed spilled

if they bury enough wild queers in the dirt
one's sure to sprout in their backyard

musk eater

kissing a stranger feels good
as leaving my hometown forever.
i do not ask his name.

in the sick, thick fog of fugue fever,
forget even the florid lure
of graffiti tunnels under the river,
lurid passage to some other patch of light.
our accents stumble over one another.
he calls the river *neckar*, though i hear *neck*.

i tell him, among the summer-sprouted
tall grass, to watch out for mosquitos,
& he hears *musk eaters*. then, he bites his lip.
i taste his blood in my mouth.

a boy without a name

invites me
into his daddy's truck.
find me, feast of forgotten
pork rinds spilled
on the floorboard.

in the parking lot,
he dances like he's high
on grease, like he's
sweat-hijacked,
holyspirit-hamstrung
between what his tongue
knows of skin's salt
& his hands
know of my throat's *yes.*

in the dream,
when i was a teen,
i was a girl
without a name.
i was a boy
without a body.
i was a tongue
starved for sugar.
i was curled
around myself
like a question mark.

i imagine myself sinking
into the river, stone-weighted.
i bob for adam apples,
bite whatever
soft flesh

lives below
the water's surface.

martyrdom of saint sebastian

after Il Sodoma

yes, once a saint pierced by arrows
survived, only to be pummeled—stained
glass skin bright & obvious as miracle
is not. one does not need to die
to be holy. he makes
a face when he comes
to the end, pretending
agony in absence of pleasure.
that's the face he wore when entered,
the shaft of an arrow penetrating
his exposed throat.

the incredulity of saint thomas
after Caravaggio

when the lord woke,
he appeared with wounds
still open on his wrists,
& his friend, in wonder
& disbelief, slid his hand
against the lord's still warm
torso, touched the gash,
born from the spear's cruel stab.

baffled, one man reaches inside another man,
& blood cleanses blood, for once.
what is alive in one man
comes alive in another.

who has not been dazzled
when slipping inside another's body,
feeling there something pulsing & alive?

white point garden, 1984

sailors, ashore for the weekend,
gather in the park after dark.
when police padlock the public restrooms,
the bushes bloom with boys on their knees.

men, some married, some too young
to know to hide their winks,
share stares too long, beckon, disappear.
they flaunt desire among cannon memorials.

air altered with pluff-mud perfume,
cars cruise in ever-closer circles.
the sea wall is no more than a stone scrim,
thin as a condom or curtain

splitting life from whatever comes after.

brief history of desire

this is tradition

interrupted:
to find one another
in cigarette-illuminated
leather bars or gaudy
motel steam rooms
fragrant with chlorine & lube.

instead, i check chat rooms, craigslist.
i download the apps & caress the screen,
blink-chirping through the night,
small sirens singing their want.

cruise-control steady,
i search for someone
whose face reminds me
of someone whose name
i can't quite recall.

in bed, i squint at the masks,
who preen & ask, *masc for masc?*
wipe glitter from my eyes,
smear my lipstick.
prune until i'm raw,
until flash-exposed flesh
bends double-over to provide
the camera phone's aperture
the best perspective of my asshole.

until later i'm broken & made whole by the same hands.

god is a sloppy kisser but a good listener

i lick dirt from god's fingernails.
god climbs into my throat,
scrapes me clean. they say,   *don't worry i like you*

                                 filthy,

                                 let me empty you. you mistake
                                 emptiness for purity.

                                 slurp the excess
                                 sweat from my neck

                                 kiss me until the salt tastes like
                                 salvation.

i don't really know the names of the flowers i massacre.

too much water, always too much much,
my mouth so full of dirt & grace.
i pluck fruit from the branch, ask about sin,

they say,   *don't you know?*
                                 everything is yours
                                 to eat. don't you know
                                 i created pleasure
                                 for you? for you.

                                 silly girl,
                                 take a bite.

aubade with baja blast spiked with gin

in the morning, sunlight oozes thin between blind slats like cheese from the edges of a quesadilla. i wake boozebamboozled, blood still sluggish with last night's clumsy desire. we territory the space between skin into something other than fear. somehow, he is still

here. i admit last night may have benefited if i had not scarfed taco bell before we made love, but listen, i didn't know he'd want to top. i didn't know he'd want to mouth my neck. listen. i didn't plan to drink so much, didn't anticipate—

the exhausted gasp spilling everything: tumult of spew, holy sphincter made uninhabitable by the passage of doritos-locos tacos one hour later. does he know what shames i have evacuated for him tonight?

i tell him about loneliness.
it is a drive-thru window & not enough change.

i am so clueless, my brief darling. it is possible to be gorgeous & still regret everything. i am trying to tell the difference between light & what light touches. i am trying to tell the difference

between how he speaks about his body
& how he speaks about mine. he tells me
it feels better to eat nothing at all, to let
the body become a hollow bell singing.

he refused even the morsel of a nacho
fry, sudden ascetic. he denied himself
every pleasure except my mouth.

slake

we are forgetful mammals,
unaware of how hair
is necessary in winter's
mouth, dark
harbor glittering
like heaven or motel sign
or salt orchard. crude
maw fixed with silver
glintwinks across the bar.
we are all throattouchbruise.
two koi, in fateful
ouroboros, attempt to keep
warm + take each other
in their mouths. gulp
summer, lurid + sweet.

mothman fucks me from behind

sing! the guttural & saccharine
taxonomy of shame:
what want demands, the body forgives.

sing! reckless want,
soft as feathered silk,
white furred skin.
contort, coax pleasure.
the spine bends like a bridge
close to collapse.

sing! glee malady
in a brokedown car parked roadside.
astonish at the wings' beating,
discover how easy awe
might be extracted from the body.
relish this epiphany of miracles
erupting under our skin.

reckless

let me be the grotto-disco queen,
the ballroom glitter-sweat
gutter-slut. filth magnet,
low maintenance pet
glass-bowled like a goldfish
perished & replaced
a dozen times by parents,
a lineage of names passed
down from the dead. toilet-flushed
guppies become anglerfish lure-light
lusting in the ocean-deep dark.

give me a careful bite, feral swallow.
peril of blood on tongue. precum-clumsy,
i'm a fawn stumbling through predawn
fog across the carolina interstate.

the splatter & guilt.
the risk i didn't have to take
in my mouth but did.

radish spirit visits the bathhouse

after Hayao Miyazaki's Spirited Away

when i lumber through steam,
eyeing the men whose gleaming bodies
stretch in shadow,
i heft no regret.

wear only the fundoshi,
ass on display. i walk
slow as sumo, salt-drenched
with a sake bowl upturned on my head.

i am never the ghost
possessed by its own hunger,
kind after being fed.
i am the mother-father monstered
into a pig after feasting.

i am the greed-gorged animal
hunkered at their feet
& kissing the soot from their soles.
i grumble my want, slobber
for the sliver of their attention.

i invite the swamp creature into bed, then set him on fire

he kisses me
mouthful of muck,
lung-emptied
like a dead cypress,
tastes the brine of my want.

i wear a wedding dress
woven of queen anne's lace
& wisteria. i slip a garter
of lichen off my thigh.

i do not recognize, at first,
the effigy of desire:
burnt moss for hair,
putrid
bog breath.

not every incandescence is beacon,
some only a house burning
or body
lit from within.

anonymous portrait

the stone bust depicts a man
long dead. he can no longer
breathe in his grave.

in the columbia museum of art,
i almost caress his cold face:
anonymous portrait.

when the greeks invade egypt,
they smash the statue's nose,
visage defaced by belief.

nose busted & bleeding,
i kneel in the dirt as a boy erases
the relief of my face from the mud.

i hold my ear to marble & listen
for the living person on the other side.
how do i enter a person, a portal?

how do i hold a stranger whose face blurs in memory?
careful, reverent.
same way i might carry an urn with ashes inside.

Part 3

For Abe

lotus eater

children sometimes
mistake yellow jessamine
for honeysuckle,
bring petals
to lips
expecting nectar,
drink instead
wasp-regret.

i once mistook
sugar for sustenance.
my teeth dropped
from my mouth,
forsaken meteors of bone.
i once mistook
meth for molly,
but swallowed
still, then stripped
out of my skin.

bite into the apple,
spit out a razor,
spit out a razed orchard.

i dissolve a pill
under a honey-serrated
tongue, surprised
at its bitter & electric.

i almost expected something sweet.

southern apocrypha with rumor
of a rodeo clown

heard it said
(secondhand, maybe)
if i were to drive a buick lesabre
seventy-miles-an-hour
toward the cliff of the ravine,
blasting dolly parton's
"island in the stream,"
i'll land
clean safe
on the other side
on the outskirts of a carnival—
no, this is a rodeo,
or at least a monster truck rally—
loud & bright enough
to make me forget
how the body feels falling
or how it might feel
slapping the surface of a shallow creek,
least that's what's been said:
i promise-land a perfect jump like that
& don't end up dead or twisted,
only garlanded with salt-rotten popcorn
& i look down at the dirt ring of the rodeo
(second rodeo, i swear)
& i see not the cowboy
who resembles every future boyfriend
i'll kiss until we don't but instead
a paint-slick fool family-familiar, almost kin
(& memory, it wavers gin-drunk like that one night i watched
brokeback mountain at three in the morning & sobbed
because it always hurts when someone dies, no matter
how many crooked elegies i scribble in my head,

& still i dream of kissing heath ledger's
beautiful dead face)
— i swear, i recognize myself down there, a ghost.
no one told me, before i painted myself a harlequin twin,
grief is a clown car we can all fit inside.

county fair

atop the ferris wheel,
the sky is black
tarmac scattered
with silver-capped
teeth lost in bar fights.
with a sloppy tongue,
i lick each star.
hold them in my cheeks
like luminescent jawbreakers.
i cannot see heaven from here,
but i can see your house.

i bounce a quarter
into the milk jug's throat.
i do not even look.
gravity does not ask
why the anvil is angry
with the bell. from here,
i make a best guess
at grief's mass.

i am envious of anyone who dies
before regret sets in.

coronation

you asked for a paper crown with your whopper, although you were turning thirty, & the teen cashier handed it over without mutiny. we took turns as monarch. onion & sweat perfumed our procession. we dropped fries into our mouths like luscious grapes, made thrones of abandoned benches, & sent imagined enemies to their deaths. you placed the flimsy circlet on my brow, & my voice dropped an octave. the crown, cartoon gold, came unclasped, crooked & sweat-wrinkled. when we polished off the bottle of stolen champagne, bubbles frothed our grease-gilded lips. this is how you left me, royal with delirium, the crown discarded under a pile of damp laundry.

months later, after you had died, i donned the crown again, discovered half-crushed behind the bookcase, cardboard soggy & peeling, crests bent forward like weary gardeners. how you left me, how you left this world, a boy king becoming suddenly older when he watched the first traitor's head roll across the floor.

what i mean when i say regret

not the match head shaved bare
in failed attempts to light the signal fire
after the plane passes over the damned island
where i've survived
the cruel innovations of wind,
specks of red sulfur & chlorate
mixing with the damp sand dunes.
no, not the sci-fi novel i abandoned
quarter-finished on the toilet tank, its heft
left to haunt me each time i brush my teeth,
until the party during which the bathroom floods
& the book becomes an insufficient sponge,
its pages wet-shredded
the same way gossamer web snaps
with the weight of morning dew.
not the nuclear-shaded soda dancing
with gin in a plastic unicorn cup
like two friends in love
who will not tell each other they're in love.
no, regret's not a corkscrew mysteriously
pierced through the skull of the man
in the hospital waiting room
the night i ambulance
you away from a lonely heaven.
regret: the wound i refuse to stitch closed myself.
the kitchen knife i steal from your bedside,
the blood i wash from the blade in the sink.

ritual for remembering that one night you were still alive

& we were lustered with joy,
gutter delight, blood cluttered
with wonder & purloined pills.

i wish i could recall
your face unblurred
by impulse.

memory is a museum with a leaky ceiling,
an archive slowly filling with water.
the artifacts become damp & indistinguishable.

a photograph deteriorates the more often it is touched.
the emulsion of this night is vinegar-sickened,
brilliant & illegible.

we stared into the sky, witnessed only
moth riot, like glitter
sweat from heaven's pores.

let me erase this evening
until only gilt remains.

the hermit

in the month after you died
by your own hand, i did not wake
without a swallow of whiskey
swishing on my tongue.
i discovered nothing
about myself
except i cannot survive
alone.

hungover

ruin electrics the air.

flood of static.
lightning excites
this liver back to life.

storm dazzles the sky
into bright hum & manic.
honey-slow bewilder.

nectar–ecstatic
hummingbirds panic
in my blood.

raptured in white noise,
a garden blooms
into blackout.

cramps erupt.
mouth turns arid
overnight. drought.

the body turns against itself,
refuses to keep anything
secret or inside.

i chase disaster with joy
or gin. i recall,
this felt good once.

~~elegy~~

you mutter with stitch
split tongue
how language
cannot salve
stab wounds
only flails
like a koi
swallowed by mud
what we write
cannot save us
only cements
what has never
existed into
permanent record
you tempt elegy
each time you open
pink & raw
as a shucked oyster
a scar is an artifact
only if you survive
what carves the scar

what is the use of words
if they only feed grief's appetite,
the use of any of this if i cannot keep you alive?

diving duck

the river's whiskey
& my body a raft
i have built from detritus.
once, i carved
an entire forest
into a canoe
just to wreck
among the rapids.
once, i swirled
deer blood
into a mural
on asphalt.
no, not a mural.
just splatter.
i am always trying
to make death
into something gorgeous.

like a wake
of buzzards
dipping beaks
into the carcass,
tearing pink kinks
of entrails
from the gut,
i am vulture-drunk
on grief.

once, a corpse
i called friend
became a poem
& i woke
with a gun

that fit perfectly
in my mouth.
once, i drank
too much gin,
then plucked an elegy
from between my teeth.

the body
decomposing
is too slow
a rapture.

how to banish a ghost

ritual is just another name for the habits
grief carves from a mourner's tongue.

you empty your mouth
until you're a rabid song

knee-sunk in your mother's garden.
prayers a rift language forgot to bridge

between bells & the human body.
did you want to die a perfect person?

every martyr dies hungry.
i never forgave you.

your anger scared me like a doe fenderstruck.
you told me about visions from god,

& i asked how a miracle was possible.
i can spit & call it ocean,

but that does not make my mouth a fount of salt.
the only thing i've ever spoken into existence

is myself, right now.
the only thing i know of god is shard-scattered in the river,

discarded jug we used to carry water home.
if i could, i swear, i would collect every piece of you.

even your milk teeth worn around my neck.
i am the relic-nostalgic apostate

asking a dead man to forgive me my blasphemy.
the debris of our joy is glorious, terrifying.

resolution

i will yearn more than i mourn. i will carry an authentic rabbit's foot. i'll stop worrying about good luck. i'll shut up the glamour racket of my heart. i will cry less. i will make non-emergency dentist appointments. i will regret nothing. i will leave this life unafraid of time. i will wake engulfed in gratitude. i will be stagnant as erosion is not. i will kiss the rain-seeped sky & slurp from dirt puddles. i will spit until i taste petrichor's bitter pluck. i will unlearn the language of sin. i will scrape shame from my tongue with a dull knife. i will surrender the old stories i've told myself to keep me alive long enough to arrive here.

some mornings, i still awake alone as a thumb
severed from a marble hand.

sloppy magician

aliveness is sleight of hand
practiced palm
card slipped   to top of deck
rehearsed flourish revealing
one hundred limp rabbits
their back left paws
          sawed for good luck

god help me   my blood's
more gin than oxygen
watch
          i will slur the words right this time

watch
          i will turn paycheck
          into puke puddle
          i will turn the body
          against itself

listen
i'm real scared of dying
          i'm real scared of living too
          let's be brave together
          —pinky promise?

          watch
          i will pull the rabbit from the hat, alive
                    intact

Part 4

the first time my nipples

throbbed after accidentally bumping
against an open door, i clasped
my chest & startled
my skin into sharp hum.
finding not yet a breast
but instead an ache-muscled
soreness, the darling promise
of transformation. water hardens,
& has always been ice.
sky tarmacs into black,
& we've never called this anything
except *night*. i am envious
of anyone who becomes
without becoming
someone else
first.

[how to build a body]

<BODY>
<TEXT>

: how wondrous <br/> this
instrument, how strange
flop atop a table <br/> wait for
storm to wake me
lightning transmutes data into
flesh <br/> softest self in
transitory sameness
Xerox replicated from
counterfeit electric
carbon copy automation

: sew feathers with glass needle

 name myself after the
smell of rain <br/> winged in-
between <br/> vessel
[breathing apparatus]
ghost <br/> coughed from the
cracked screen <br/> machine
in the image of ~~man~~

: ERROR ERROR ERROR

<define: BODY>

: simulacra of sparked synapse
: collapse-prone architecture
: accident of bond-tipsy electrons
: outdated appliance
: used model
: ancient technology

: artificial grief avatar
: clustered codex of cellular ruin
: sepulcher of synthetic skin
: invention with faulty circuits
: split-screen desire manifest
: unmiracle
: brilliant bone origami
: the first mistake

camouflage practice

i don a dress
same way some men
polish a casket
before burying
their fathers inside
whatever stories
they tell about their fathers.

i name this glitter sacrament,
eyeliner an ancient ritual unearthed.
i imagine fingernail polish
as red-dyed grease in the blood,
recipe for disaster passed down.

knot lace tight as a clenched fist.
here, elegance is survival technique.

ecological survey on genderfluid species

when a cardinal displays
both red & brown-gray pigment,
this is called bilateral gynandromorph.

marsh harriers,
in subtle drag,
turn gray feathers to brown.

in the egg,
at high temperatures,
bearded dragons femme.

banana slugs fuck
in ouroborus,
boasting twin genitals.

clown fish transition,
& so do sea bass.
hawkfish change sex at will.

it is simple to dissect
what is infeasible,
easy to slice,

to disembowel, to disembody, to disregard

with clean taxonomy,
to correct nomenclature,
to ensure proper analysis.

i abhor surviving in a stranger's mouth, clenched
between teeth like a squirming nymph-larva
pinned by budding wings to the page.

i want only to remember i am animal
haunting the body of an animal.

the fruit archive

inheritance is the incorrect word
for the righteous pulse that stutters
when i learn of this history,
how the story spills
teeth on asphalt.
each document in the fruit archive
is a red-soaked landscape,
a forget-compass
leaving blank spots on the map.

under every map,
queer topography— secret as joy & ancient
as erosion. i find brilliant pebbles
speckled with blood, evidence
that someone once was alive
carving desires into stone.

stone shelves worn, chipped
like a brick thrown back,
stacked with mason jars:
preserved queer fruits
still bruised from harvest.
the water rises,
brief flood
swelling tomes
into indecipherable violence,
river-urgent end of a heterosexual reign.

rain seeps through the ceiling of the fruit archive,
riot of seeds splitting open easy as a skull.
the dirt is bloodwet & blooming rage,
& here, even drowning
in what is never said aloud,
i find a worthy inheritance.

martyrdom of saint sebastian

after Guido Reni

look closer. don't mistake
tree trunk for Wyoming fencepost,
saint for boy, though in the end,
they died the same, beaten, blued,
bloated & abandoned.
but in this moment, hands bound
over his head, eyes toward heaven,
he's still alive. shot through
with light. throat exposed
like a shepherd giving
his life over to wolves.

sacrifice

in the beginning, a small lamb
split open upon an altar, blood
spilled from a body still
warm. this is how some men worship,
a father's blade against the neck of a boy,
his son a vessel of obedient sin.

how else to cleanse sin
except to slaughter the lamb?
gushwarm as the thigh of a boy.
a body bathed in another's blood
learns how to properly worship,
shudders, gasps, then goes still.

what remains still
is the question of where sin
seeps when the body ceases worship,
how even what is ruined becomes lamb
when cleansed in blood,
a field of limbwrecked boys.

the splatter of a boy
becomes bloodborne warship.
he grasps my head like a sacrificial lamb.
i clean my face & still
taste the sour tart of sin,
metallic, almost like blood.

a new song enters the blood,
cleanses the body in antithesis to worship.
how miraculous the factory of sin,
what slips in through the boy's
mouth, corrupts every organ until stilled.
an altar without a lamb.

controlled burn

home: landscape set ablaze.
field sown with ash, bone.
feathers singed by sun.
sons eclipsed by flame.
harbor of ghost ships
flickers, burns bright,
memorial to mourn
the lost lisp, the forgotten
name, the forlorn body.

in oakland, the fire
in a warehouse,
temporary shelter
becomes home tangled
in wires, like kudzu slithering
into a verdant field.

in new orleans,
the upstairs lounge
blazed in a douse
of lighter fluid,
& those who escaped
fell through the barred windows
still burning.

in dallas, two men
immolated in their home.
the police reported,
not a hate crime,
not a pyre to which to pray,
not a priority.

this: smoke-disastered
eulogy we cannot hear

until we press
our ears against
a closed door,
a horror of hot tongues
humming a sermon-hymn,
music louder than hunger.

the trans archive self-immolates

when one buries fruit,
it does not always bloom.

ash mistaken for dirt.

i can trace the border
of a field with my finger
& tell myself *here.*
i can smudge orange crayon,
misname the flicker of a boy,
will-o-wisp flitting in the dark.

we can dig until our hands
bloody with the surprise
of rumor becoming history.
the map is not the terror story.

violence is never true
unless someone writes it down.
every ghost also a threat
to place my body underground.

the girl drowned,
but no one tells which hands
held her under.
the boy burned,
but no one tells who lit the match.

i am trying so hard to remember,
to recover anything as proof,
but i'm getting the details wrong,
rearranging strips of torn newspaper
with only an uncertain tongue.

i'm like a child rubbing
gravestones with chalk,
trying desperately to transcribe
but still slowly eroding the names.

on the question, "wait, can trans women reclaim the word *faggot?*"

i've been called a faggot
enough times to know
the origin of the word,
which refers to kindling
used in fires, which refers
to queer bodies used as
kindling. last time a man
shouted this to me, i was
drunk outside of a bar. i
misheard him & asked,
wait, forget what?

forget   shame,   silly
protestations of protestant
upbringing. forget i like it
when they beat my ass
blue with a bible. forget
the   boy   whose   lit
cigarette once singed a
perfect circle on my skin.
forget violence is relative,
that i wake each morning
in a warm bed. forget to
play dead, roadkill song
clenched in my teeth,
forget

my teeth, their bite, the thumb hooked
in my mouth, angling for
affection. forget desire
is   salmon   in   the
bloodstream spilling into

yes. forget even this in parade of searching hands, soft bellies. forget shame, damn it, am i not yet bored of shame? forget pleasure can be pleasurable.   forget pretending to be radical & queer on twitter. forget the woman who while reading out loud the names of murdered trans women at the stonewall inn fifty years after the riot was shushed by a crowd of white gay men for ruining their fun.

we do not need to remember the origin of the word, how what is twinebound   & bodytwinned will burn easy.

we will only forget.

chandelier

after Antonio Salviati

i'm wearing a sequined dress at the new year's party, conspicuous as a supernova. my beard's unkempt, not yet abandoned, the only makeup a slash of sloppy eyeliner. someone asks if i'm in drag, & i wanna say something smart. i wanna quote judith butler, but i've never actually read judith butler.

in 2018, rupaul revealed he would not accept openly transitioning transgender contestants to participate on *drag race*.

the candelabra, invented during the medieval period, is replaced in immense spaces (abbeys, chapels, feasting halls) with chandeliers to provide better illumination, but also as a symbol of wealth. their crystal is an opulent wink.

the first time i ever attend a drag show, the queen lip syncs ke$ha because it is 2012 & everyone lip-syncs ke$ha. she threatens to topple in ten-inch killer heels. she's a glam-damned double dare in a dress. she sashays across a dirty stage, torch-lush ritual. i do not syntax desire into genderfucked sense. i am pure spectator, all eyes & awe.

the first time i hear the word *gay*, someone describes a boy tied to a fence post & beaten to death.

in the soviet union, some factories were assessed on how much material they used to construct products, & often chandeliers from those factories were overweighted, threatening always to crash onto the heads of the dancing pairs in russian ballrooms.

as a child, i cannot stop wondering when a piano will fall from the sky, like they do in cartoons. i am not safe here, not anywhere.

in 2013, i meet a gay opera singer who serenades a huddle of men in an apartment in havana. his voice is fragile & gorgeous as flint glass. months later, i learn, he's been shot in the street. i don't know why.

nothing beautiful is safe for long.

the chandelier hanging in the columbia museum of art is a crown of colored glass, curlicued with flowers pink-dawn tinged. hand-blown & hotworked in the 1880s by antonio salviati. the glass is a fireworks-splatter of red, orange, blue.

drag, before paraded by mostly cis men in rupaul's shadow, was developed in the ballroom scene by black and latina trans queens. these were ballrooms without chandeliers but still plenty of light.

the first time i hear the word *genderfluid*, i hear also the story of a teenager found in an alley, two bullet holes in the head, gagged & hooded with a trash bag, body doused with bleach.

when i visit the columbia museum of art, i sit on the floor & imagine dismantling the artifice from the ceiling, shattering sculpted flint glass until elegance becomes dangerous. each shard a translucent dagger sharp enough to hold to a throat.

i put on the dress, brittle, glittering taboo.

i promise to curse strangers into inarticulate stutter.

i am too old to still be afraid of becoming whatever i am. i am too old to be learning new things about my body.

in the cartoon about falling pianos, the instrument is also vessel for symphony.

at the new year's party, they ask again if i'm in drag. i try to quote judith butler & say gender is a performance i've never been super good at. i tell them, i have been dreaming of becoming a chandelier instead.

ablaze, far from here, & safe.

i am searching for a place that feels safe.

tres(passing)

each day is trespass, the horizon
an electric fence flickering threat.
each day scattered buckshot, a split mouth
knit closed with respectable salutation.
you must pass as someone who comes from the dirt,
or else get buried underneath the dirt.
i decide to stay another year,
to carve a home, to hum the trans body
into a song that belongs here.

yes i've seen the future & i promise i'm still alive,

still paying
out of pocket
for hormones
still opulent
when cascaded
with opalescent
plastic pearls
thrifted for three dollars
still painting
nails that blue razz
that pops
like a tongue
only capable
of cooking eggs
& when i wipe
my brow
with greased fingers
pimples erupt
like adolescent
devil horns
still shaving
every day, so close
my lips crimson
still looking
for the perfect-sized bralette
except by now
my tits
have grown
into more
than fresh fat
on my chest
i cup

new breasts
in the mirror
& examine
the vessel
i have become
i am translated
most simply
as constellation
cluster of stars
with a name
i've chosen myself
i ache
i break open
& like water
abandon form
i carve
my feminine name
the same way
a river fissures
rock into ravine
slow and deliberate:
      oh! Evelyn, where have we been?

Notes

The "you" that appears in several poems is in reference to a friend named Abe, who died from suicide in 2020. Many of these poems are written in mourning of him.

Several poems in this collection reference my dead name. I chose to explicitly include this name so as not to create a veil of shame around a name I used for the majority of my life, a past version of myself with whom I would like to cultivate a relationship of care and compassion.

"i'm seven when i dredge" references the train crash in Graniteville, South Carolina on January 6, 2005, when derailed rail cars released chlorine gas that resulted in the death of nine people and hospital admissions for over 500.

"still," "anonymous portrait," and "chandelier" were originally written as part of an ekphrastic poetry series for the Columbia Museum of Art. The painting described in "still" is *Still Life* (1657) by Pieter Claesz, the marble bust described in "anonymous portrait" is *Anonymous Portrait Bust* (mid-300s Roma), and the chandelier in "chandelier" was created by Antonio Salviati (1880s).

"iva!" is dedicated to Iva Reed-Manes, an abstract painter, photographer, and my best friend.

"boyhood: revisions" include two video game references: the Konami code, a cheat code used in the Nintendo game *Contra* (1987) and in-game dialogue from *Pokemon Red/Blue* (1998).

The title "musk eater" is inspired by a quote from ecologist Dr. Ruth Patrick, who overheard a Southern-accented guard refer to mosquitoes as "musk eaters" during an ecological survey of the Savannah River. This account is recorded in *Savannah River Site at Fifty* (2000).

Two poems entitled "martyrdom of saint sebastian" appear in this collection, the first an ekphrastic of the painting by Il Sodoma and the second of the painting by Guido Reni. Saint Sebastian is often revered as the gay saint, well-loved by queer writers and painters throughout history. The second poem references Matthew Shepard, who was brutally murdered for being gay in Laramie, Wyoming in 1998.

The poem "white point garden, 1984" refers to a public park in Charleston, South Carolina colloquially known as "battery park." In the early 1980s, the park became a popular cruising spot, especially for sailors visiting the harbor. This history is recorded in Harlan Greene's book *The Real Rainbow Row: Explorations of Charleston's LGBTQ History* (2022).

"radish spirit visits the bathhouse" reimagines the minor character Radish Spirit from Hayao Miyazaki's *Spirited Away* (2001) as visiting a gay bathhouse rather than one for spirits.

"the hermit" was written as a part of a series of ekphrastic poems in response to the seventy-eight cards of the tarot. Additional poems that drew from this series include "on the third day," "resolution," and "i've seen the future & i promise i'm still alive,".

"diving duck" borrows its title and first line from the song "If the River was Whiskey (Divin' Duck Blues)" by Charlie Poole and the Rising Sons.

"[how to build a body]" borrows its form from computer coding languages.

"sacrifice" is a truncated sestina, a revised form suggested by Melissa Crowe when the poem was first published in *Beloit Poetry Journal.*

"controlled burn" refers to a series of fires, including an accidental fire at Ghost Ship in Oakland, California in 2016, an arson attack at The

Upstairs Lounge in New Orleans, Louisiana in 1973, and an arson attack that killed two gay men in their apartment in Dallas, Texas in 2011.

"Chandelier" includes a reference to a 2018 interview with RuPaul on excluding trans women from the reality TV show *Drag Race*: "You can identify as a woman and say you're transitioning, but it changes once you start changing your body." As of 2024, more than a dozen trans contestants have competed on the show.

Acknowledgements

Versions of these poems appeared in the following journals:

Anti-Heroin Chic: "southern apocrypha with rumor of a rodeo clown"

Barely South Review: "i'm seven when i dredge a cold body from the creek"

beestung: "Chandelier"

Beloit Poetry Journal: "sacrifice"

Blue Mountain Review: "sloppy magician"

BOAAT: "lotus eater"

buggery (chapbook published by Bateau Press, received the BOOM chapbook prize 2019/2020): "god is a sloppy kisser, but a good listener," "slake," "reckless," and "white point garden, 1984"

Carolina Muse: portions of "iva!"

Day Job Journal: "summer of the push mower"

Drunk Monkeys: "coronation"

Fall Lines: "house show" and "ritual superstition"

Fatal Flaw Magazine: "yes i've seen the future and i promise i'm still alive"

Gigantic Sequins: "elegy"

Impossible Archetype: "on the question 'wait, can trans women reclaim the word *faggot?*'" and "radish spirit visits the bathhouse"

Jasper Writes: "genderfluent" and "ecological survey on genderfluid species"

Jet Fuel Review: "diving duck"

Lackadaisy: "county fair"

Lemonstar Magazine: "praise song in lieu of obituary"

Longleaf Review: "mothman fucks me from behind"

Pidgeonholes: "hungover"

Raleigh Review: "we've got wilderness stuck in our teeth"

Running with Water (an anthology): "musk eater"

Sandhills: "still" and "southern ecology"

Sledgehammer Lit: "what you mean when you say regret"

South Carolina Review: "the trans archive self-immolates"

Split Rock Review: "[how to build a body]"

Susurrus Magazine: "controlled burn"

Taco Bell Quarterly: "aubade with baja blast spiked with gin"

underblong: "iva!"

Weekly Hubris: "martyrdom of saint sebastian (after guido reni)," "queer the smear," "a boy without a name," and "i invite the swamp creature into bed then set him on fire"

Yemassee: "camouflage practice"

Zingara Poetry Review: "the fruit archive"

Thank You

This book has been made possible by generous funding through a creative writing fellowship from the National Endowment for the Arts.

This manuscript was partially revised and rewritten at the Sundress Academy for the Arts Residency in the Writer's Coop at Firefly Farms.

Thank you to Sundress Publications for ushering this book into the world and helping shape this into its best possible form. Special thanks to my editor Erin Elizabeth Smith.

Thank you Barrett Warner, a mentor and friend, who offered invaluable insight on a previous version of this manuscript.

Thank you to writing groups that have offered feedback and community, including Poetry Society of South Carolina, South Carolina Writers Association, Savannah River Poets, The Unspoken Word, and The Guild of Poetic Intent.

I want to give thanks to a community of mentors and peers, including Marcus Amaker, Han VanderHart, Moses Oaktree, Corozon Stegelin, Jenny Ree Gilmore, Anna Norris, Loren Mixon, Miho Kinnas, Matthew Robertson, Ed Madden, Lisa Hase Jackson, Linda J. Walder, and all of my creative friends in Charleston, Columbia, Greenville, Aiken, and Augusta.

Special thanks to the staff at New Moon Cafe in Aiken, South Carolina, where I revised countless versions of this manuscript.

Thank you to Iva Reed Manes, my best friend, for keeping me here.

Thank you to Alex Bishop, love of my life.

About the Author

Evelyn Berry (she/her) is a trans author, editor, and educator from South Carolina. She is the recipient of a 2023 National Endowment for the Arts creative writing fellowship, 2020 BOOM Chapbook Prize from Bateau Press, 2019 Broad River Prize for Prose, and 2018 Emrys Poetry Prize, among other honors. Her work has appeared in *Beloit Poetry Journal, Gigantic Sequins, beestung, Raleigh Review, Taco Bell Quarterly*, and elsewhere. This is her debut poetry collection.

Other Sundress Titles

Slaughterhouse for Old Wives Tales
Hannah V Warren
$16

Age of Forgiveness
Caleb Curtiss
$16

Where My Umbilical is Buried
Amanda Galvan-Huynh
$16

In Stories We Thunder
V. Ruiz
$16

Slack Tongue City
Mackenzie Berry
$16

Sweetbitter
Stacey Balkun
$16

Cosmobiological
Jilly Dreadful
$20

Dad Jokes from Late in the Patriarchy
Amorak Huey
$16

Nocturne in Joy
Tatiana Johnson-Boria
$16

Another Word for Hunger
Heather Bartlett
$16

Little Houses
Athena Nassar
$16

the Colored page
Matthew E. Henry
$16

Year of the Unicorn Kidz
jason b. Crawford
$16

Something Dark to Shine In
Inès Pujos
$16

Slaughter the One Bird
Kimberly Ann Priest
$16

The Valley
Esteban Rodriguez
$16